I0098258

The Sun
Will Rise
Tomorrow

Copyright 2019 by Kim McCaskey

All rights reserved. No part of this book may be reproduced or transmitted in any form or by any means, electronic or mechanical, including photocopying recording, or by any information storage and retrieval system without written permission from the publisher or the author. The only exception is brief quotations for reviews.

For information address:

J2B Publishing LLC
4251 Columbia Part Road
Pomfert, MD 20675
www.J2BLLC.com
GladToDoIt@gmail.com

Cover Photo: Sunrise over Mansfield on Lake Champlain taken from the Crater Club, Essex, NY. James Burd Brewster, 2017

Printed and bound in the United States of America

ISBN: 978-1-948747-62-2

The Sun
Will Rise
Tomorrow

Kim McCaskey

J2B Publishing

Dedication

This book is dedicated, with love, to my children, my husband and my dog. My kids provided me a purpose in life when they came into this world. My husband sees what is in my heart and always believes in me. And last, but not least, my dog has given me a true understanding of unconditional love.

Table of Contents

Children

A Son

A son is the joy of his mother's eye
She held him, loved him and soothed his cry
There's no greater love between a mother and son
They understand each other more than anyone

He's the boy she molded into a man
Lifting him up and telling him he can
She loved him and prayed for him throughout the years
She watched his mistakes and hid her fears

A mom is the one who is the love of his life
And she knows that will change when he takes a wife
That's the time when she must let go
Let him be a man and let him grow

For there will come a time when the mom will grow old
She will need his help and his hand to hold
This strong and faithful man
Will lift her up and tell her she can

Loving and praying for her throughout the years
Watching her make mistakes and hiding his fears
A son is always a mother's very best friend
Remaining her little boy to the very end

Teach A Child

Teach a child to always be kind
And they will never forget

Teach a child to give and not take
And they will always be rich

Teach a child to tell the truth
And they will always be wise

Teach a child to not judge others
And they will always have friends

Teach a child to appreciate what they have
And they will always give

Teach a child to love and be loved
And they will never feel alone

Teach a child to have a voice
And they will always be heard

Teach a child to like who they are
And they will have a good life

Teach a child mistakes are just lessons
And the lessons will be learned

Teach a child to do what they say
And they will go far

Teach a child all these things
And it's a job well done

After College

After college
What do I do?
Classes are over
What should I pursue?

No all-nighters
Not one more test
Do I have to get a real job?
And be like the rest?

Goodbye frat parties, formals and bars
So long pizza, beer and weed
Adios, study groups
It's my time to lead

I will miss my freedom
I will miss all the fun
I'd like to stay four more years
But my parents say I am done!

To the Bride of My Son...

The day has finally come
That I am no longer number one
To the little boy I've so loved
Whom I proudly call my son

I knew God would bring you
I knew he would choose wise
I knew you would love him
By the look in your eyes

I've seen my son grow
Into a wonderful man
I've watched you support him
And tell him he can

You see the goodness
He has in his heart
And the kind person he is
From the very start

I tried my best
To raise him right
To teach him manners
And to be polite

He's never failed me
Though he's made some mistakes
I've seen him turn his life around
And do what it takes

To someday be a loving husband
A father, a friend
To love you forever
To the very end

So, my wish for you
His beautiful bride
Is patience, forgiveness, honesty and trust
And may you stand strong forever, side by side

The Better Part of Me

The better part of me
Was given freely
On the day you were born

It's like you saw within me
The person I am
But will never be

Did you hear my prayers?
Feel my passion?
Understand my dreams?

My wish to you
Before we met
Was for you to be
The better version of me

The mistakes I made
The opportunities I passed
The people I hurt
Would never be who you are

I loved you,
I nurtured you,
I told you how great you would be

Finally, the day came
That I held you in my arms and looked into your eyes
Feeling so much love in my heart

I knew I did right
Because you are
The better part of me

Hope

Be

Be alive

Be present

Be thankful

Be grateful

Be happy

Be radiant

Be compassionate

Be warm

Be playful

Be inspiring

Be a reason

Be a solution

Be there

Be a friend

Be somebody

Be beautiful

Be, the state of being

Be, the top-level domain

Be

The Sun Will Rise Tomorrow

Today didn't go well

Beginning with the blare of the alarm

Another monotonous day lingering ahead

Hesitation on my part to get out of bed

Obligations await me

My mind tells me to get up

Yet, I don't budge

I turn off the alarm

Rolling over on my side

The darkness of the room

Engulfs me into no space or time

My brain tries to pick up

On the dream I was just having

And I slip into it easily

My dream is reoccurring

It always knocks on the door

Of my consciousness

Never, do I answer the door freely

But it's a rude, pushy, unwelcome visitor

Barging into my realm

Whether I like it or not

The dream replays over and over

On the screen behind my eyes

My body becomes restless

And the tightness in my chest

Is enclosing my heart

Making me relive the pain

A sob escapes from my lips

Why can't I rewind this part of my life?
Rewrite the script

The way I wanted it to end

You never leaving me

As a shattered version of what I use to be

Why can't you love me?

Am I just not enough?

I can't seem to move on or let you go

Yet, I'm just a fleck of time in your past

Someone you might recollect now and again

I question my existence

Why am I even here?

The only thing of certainty

Is the sun will rise tomorrow

The Seasons of My Life

The seasons of my life
Are fresh and stark and new
Bringing hope to my mind
Foreshadowing the things to come
In all the colors we expect
Sometimes hard to predict
If the seasons will be mild or harsh
My winter comes as depression
The cold, the gray, the blues
Feeling like a life sentence
Until spring comes into view
The signs of spring remind us
That life will start again
Letting go of the past
And opening the door to the warm breeze of summer
Summer is my happy place
I feel free, excited and young
Enjoying the lull of the time of year
Savoring the heat upon my skin
Fall, the beautiful array of hues
Brings sadness as the leaves begin to plummet
The world around me perishes once more
A season of my life in full circle

What's Over the Rainbow?

Out of nowhere

The most spectacular sight

Appears across the sky

A vibrant band of color

Gift from God

Reminder of His promise

Excitement flows

Closed eyes

Wish made

A smile

A giggle escapes the lips

Childhood thought of a pot of gold

And the dream that you dare

For a fleeting moment

Reality is put aside

The walk across the celestial bridge

Quickly turns into a run

A run from your troubles today

A run to a new beginning

Beautiful mirage in the distance

Springtime

The doors open up
To the beauty of life
A season of new starts
Rebirth
You can smell it in the air
The toll of a harsh winter
Is long gone
The dismal brown landscape
Slowly starts to change
The cool breeze
Brings promises of days to come
More daytime than night
The trees come alive
It's time to come out of hiding
Listen...
Did you hear the distant call?
Of the cardinal sitting on the fence
Shouting it's time to come out
Instantly, a melody of warble
Clamors through the sky
The hour is here
Wake up
Delight in God's beauty
Open your windows
Let the sunshine in
A season of transformation
Inhale the splendor of spring!

Lessons

A Good Kick in the A**

There are times in our life
That we all need a good kick in the a**
And that means everyone
No one gets a pass

It might come from a father, a mother, a coach
A person trying to guide you on the right track
And help you get rid of that egotistical sass
Even if this means it will hold you back

By showing you the ropes and calling you out
Hold you responsible to own your mistakes
Not letting you argue and pass the blame
To do the right thing, whatever it takes

The kick usually comes swift and it comes fast
It stings, it hurts, it bruises your ego
Your temper rises and you are ready to blow
But the seed is planted, and it will begin to grow

One day you will look back and thank your friend
For the much-needed kick in your seat
The lesson was learned and taken to heart
It's time to move on and never repeat

Alone

There is a difference
Between being alone
And being lonely
You're ok with being alone
It's a period in your life
That requires you to look inside
Yet, so many are afraid
Of being alone
Scared of the silence
Or of what they might find
Maybe it's the word "one"
Inside of alone
Fearing you will always be just one
But to me, one represents you
The "one" God created
Not another "one" alike
Take some time to be alone
Sometime in your life
To fall in love with who you really are
Change the things that need to be
And get in "one" with yourself

Confucius say...

Show respect
Honor your elders
Look at the "Big Picture"
Beyond Heaven
Pay attention
To what is being sent
The wise man
Knows the difference
Between good and evil
Study
Past to present
Learn from both
Hone your mind
Reason
Pursue yourself
Don't conform
Not too much
Not too little
Be a thinker
Be understood
Make your own Destiny
Love yourself
Love others
Do the right thing
Because it's the right thing
To do
Find the beauty
In all things
That's what
Confucius say...

Humble

Humble is the definition
Of what it means
To be
A truly powerful
Human Being

Let Go of the Ego

There is a purpose within
Each and every one of us
That the ego holds prisoner
Locked behind doors
Of insecurity and fear
Afraid of challenges and failures
Now is the time
To live in the present moment
What's your soul's purpose?
Break free
Seek the unknown
Find out who you really are
The transformation
Just takes awareness
Safety, Security
A sense of belonging
Experiencing this spiritual awakening
Empowers you

No Means No

If someone says no

There is no reason to argue

Or force yourself upon them

And disrespect their space

It doesn't matter

If they are tipsy

Drunk

Depressed or blue

If someone says no

Then it is up to you

To respect their wishes

Their body

Their mind

If you walk away from the situation

You are both winners

Own It

Don't put the blame
On someone else
It isn't fair to them
It's not their game

Be true to yourself
Admit what you've done
Not being true to you
Is detrimental to your health

Swallow your pride
Get down on your knees
Ask for forgiveness
You already lied

When you do what's right
It's for the win
Own it, man
Keep fighting the good fight!

Tis The Reason

Scurrying around
Like a mouse in a maze
Trying to find the perfect gifts
Caught up in the buying craze

Who is coming?
Do we have time to make mass?
Is the eggnog too strong?
Will it kick your ass?

Time is running out
A sense of overwhelm is setting in
The big kids want cash
So, it's a win-win

To cook or to cater?
Which shall it be?
Are the gifts all wrapped?
Should they be put under the tree?

The cookies are made
The table is lovely
Hors d'oeuvres are planned
To be served with bubbly

Will everyone eat ham?

Must there be a vegan menu?

Why at our house?

Should we find a bigger venue?

The stress is too much

This is no longer fun

I don't want to host

I'm ready to run

Why doesn't the rest of the family offer?

Can't they take over for this season?

Does anyone step up?

What is the reason?

Well, my friends, I've figured it out

We've lost the spirit of this special day

Instead of the hustle, the bustle, the shopping, the stress

It's time to slow down, be grateful, and pray

Feeling Blue

Drowning

Slowly sinking

Like a penny

You put into a glass of water

The sight is graceful

The loose form twirling

To the bottom

You are watching in slow motion

An outsider looking in

There is an empty numbness

Gaze set straight forward

A warmth surrounds your body

But a sudden chill creeps in

The struggle is real

In the moment

Are you strong enough?

Contemplation sets in

To sink or swim?

Only you have the answer

The will

The will to sink or swim

Don't let your story

Be one of those

Lost at sea

Hurtful Words

Hurtful words never solve a thing

They come out too fast

And slash their victim

For a fleeting moment

It makes the giver

Feel empowered

But the receiver

Bleeds

You win

Saturday Blues

I rub my temples
As if that will make the feeling go away
My mind wonders…

There is a tension throughout my body
Boredom, Unease, Discontentment
It's hard to pinpoint

Or give it a name
It will come and go
Like an unwelcome visitor for the weekend

Showing up out of nowhere
Expecting to be entertained
I'm waiting for,

I'm waiting for…
My mind to wonder
The tension to ease from my body

Excitement, Peace, Fulfillment
It's hard to pinpoint
Or give it a name

I think I will call it "Saturday Blues"

Scared

That

Reality

Eliminates

Someone's

Self

Fixations

A Love-Hate Relationship with Food

I enjoy it

My downfall, my weakness

Food is my passion

My pastime, my enjoyment

Evoking a feeling of pleasure

And a feeling of guilt

They coincide with each other

Occupying a space in my brain

The right and left hemisphere

The left being my sense of reason

While the right creatively justifies my indulgence

It's like having a secret lover

That you cannot wait to embrace

You don't want anyone to know about the affair

Savoring the moment

Engulfing the smells, textures, tastes

Stirring me into a euphoric state

Cheese

Cheese oh cheese

I love you so much

I can't give you up

As much as I want

Cheese oh cheese

You make me feel so good

With your yellow tones

And creamy insides

Cheese oh cheese

How do we break this off?

You really aren't good for me

You are tasty, but not nice

Cheese oh cheese

I am ready to replace you

No more Cheddar, Swiss, Gouda, or Colby

I have decided on my new vice

Vodka on ice

Habit

I am not a person of habit
I turn off the alarm before it rings
I jump out of bed
Head for the potty
Feed the dog
Do my morning stretches
Let out the dog
Grab a cup of coffee
Turn on the news
Put on my makeup
Fix my hair
Brush my teeth
Get dressed
Make the bed
Pack my lunch
Refill coffee
Do a morning prayer
Kiss my husband
Pet the dog
Check the clock
7:27 a.m.
Jump in the car
Head to work
Whew, thank goodness
I'm so flexible

MONEY

MORE, MORE, MORE

$ $ $ $ $

NEVER ENOUGH

$ $ $ $ $

WHO WANTS TO LIVE ON A BUDGET?

$ $ $ $ $

The Perfect Tan

The sun beats on my skin
On a hot summer day
I'm hoping the flesh of winter
Will quickly fade away

A sun goddess by day
Skin is glowing by night
After a quick shower
My body is neon bright

My youth is shining before me
There is intensity from the heat of the rays
I feel confident in my skin
I've been working on this sun kissed look for days

Maybe my fix is fleeting
I know I'm risking my youthful beauty
When I lay out in the sun
And my skin takes this beating

But the sun feels so good
I doubt I will ever stop
I'm a Leo, ruled by the sun
It's a habit I will never drop!

My Best Friend, Joe

Joe greets me every morning

Rain or shine

Good day or bad day

Never judging me

Or asking questions

Just calmly waiting

To put a smile on my face

And make me feel alive

And energetic

Likewise, I don't judge Joe

By his color

Or his body

Or his smell

Or his nationality

I just take him, on most occasions

In small doses

Unless it's a tough day

And then I must rely on Joe

To help me focus and recharge

And get through the day

But I must admit

Too much of Joe

Isn't healthy for me

He can make me irritated

Upset my stomach

And completely stress me out

But I will never end my relationship with Joe

Some may think I'm addicted to Joe

I probably am

There are worse vices though

I need Joe in my world

He is my liquid energy

My cupped lightening!

Love

Crosswords

I love crosswords
The puzzles make me think
I'm no dictionary

The Love of a Dog

Nothing can beat the love of your child,
But the love of a dog is a different animal

They show you their affection with the lick of their tongue,
Wanting nothing in return

A companion, a friend, a confidante, a faithful listener
Never telling any of your secrets

Sensing when something isn't right, your dog is the first to
know
The first to comfort, the last to judge

They will never let you go to bed alone or eat by yourself
They are the best left-over eater and floor cleaner upper ever

A toothy smile can melt your heart
A slobbery kiss lifts you up

But the best of the best for owning a dog
Is the feeling of a "Rock Star" when you walk in the door!

Soul Mate

Given to you
From the Lord above
Not expected
No arrival date
Just a gift
A perfect present
Custom made
Designed to fit
Meant to last
Someone you've met
Each night in your dreams
Suddenly
Your reality is real
Deep down inside
A fire burns bright
With the intensity and fire
That brings you alive
Gaze into their eyes
What do you see?
Insecurity?
Intimacy?
Confidence?
Compassion?
Twin Flames
Destined from the Universe
A feeling of de'ja'vu

The Sea

The sea
To me
Is the best place to be
The sand between my toes
Makes me forget my woes
As my mind slows

The sun radiating on my face
In this massive space
Puts me in my happy place
That is the sea
To me

The Sun

Warm upon my skin
Radiating from above
Making me feel good

To You, My Husband

These words, my husband,
Are straight from my heart
I knew I loved you
From the very start
There was something about your crooked smile
And rugged charm
I felt the immediate attraction
When your hand brushed against my arm
Time seemed to stop
When I looked into your dark eyes
So deep, so rich, flooded with kindness
Noble, steadfast, very wise
My feelings for you
Have deepened each and everyday
As the man you are unfolds
And amazes me in every way
You are my rock, my reason, my light
The person I turn to, the person I trust
The one I reach for throughout the night
I waited a long time
For you to enter my life
There has never been a moment
I have regretted becoming your wife
So, you my lover, my friend, my mate
We have so much to look forward to

So much to see and learn

We get the great opportunity to grow old together

All because of that very first date

Fun

My Stomach

It growls

It bangs

It churns

It turns

I ignore it

It bloats

It aches

It burns

It begs

I feed it

Necktie

Why is it so hard
for a man to tie a tie?
They wind it
They loop it
They even go around
But it never looks quite right
Why?
Just tie!

Sinfully Good

Foul smelling Limburger Cheese

Bad Ass Marine

Mean pair of jeans

Sickening case of puppy love

Naughty lingerie

Wicked, The Musical

Ungodly amount of money

Devilish good looks

Decadent chocolate cake

Uncontrolled laughter

Damn good woman

Fearsome love of God

Guilty!

Relaxations

A Good Class of Wine

Brings joy to my lips
Red, white, dry, sparkling
I'm not really picky
Price isn't a dilemma
As long as my glass is full
Conversation will carry forward
Through sips

Butterfly

                                  Butterfly

Beautiful and shy
Quietly flying around
Landing gracefully
Never harming anyone
The elegance of a butterfly

Butterfly

          Butterfly

Clink, Clink

At the end of a long day
I kick up my feet
Ah, the cool feel of leather on my legs
Sitting next to me
Within my reach
A glass on the table
Five cubes, to be exact
Ice slowly melting
Infusion of perfection
Bourbon of choice
I pick up my friend
Give my hand a shake
Clink, clink
Cheers to me!

Free

To be one's self

Not owned by anyone

Flying high with thoughts and notions

Unlocking hidden treasures

Kept in a sacred place

Where no one has a key

Its meaning is very exclusive

Not many can define it

Exploring, creating, dreaming, doing

No worries

No stress

No pleasing

Just running the race

And not caring who wins

Laughter

God's gift to us

The rebirth of our soul

Each time we partake

In the joy of a good laugh

It is written in His book

Reminding us not to take this life

So seriously

Have a good laugh

Even if it's laughing

At yourself

You will live longer

Starring as the comedian

In your own show

Highway Therapy

There is something about the open road

Sleek and black

An open invitation

To a destiny unknown

That clears your mind

The tight grip on the steering wheel

Brings delight

In a way removed from the everyday mundane

Mindlessly you stare ahead

Letting the car

Navigate between the lines

Remnants of the past

Speeding by

Should you slow down

Stop or turn around

And go back?

The caution sign in the distance

Brings you back to reality

Back to the road

There's no turning around at this point

Not an exit in sight

Gazing into the rear mirror

Reflects where you've been

And what you have just passed

Slowly becoming smaller and smaller

Your arm begins to relax

And you become aware of the song

On the radio

"Who Says You Can't Go Home"

On a Beautiful Day

On a beautiful day
Everything seems right
Not a worry in my mind
With the sun shining so bright

The long gray winter
Took a toll on my soul
But the vivid blue sky
Makes me alive and whole

I close my eyes
And inhale the crisp air
Thanking God for His beauty
In a heart-felt prayer

My body begins to relax
My heart starts to glow
I'm feeling the love
I want everyone to know

That I savor these days
I don't want them to end
Tomorrow will come
Until we meet again, my friend

Thoughts

2020 Resolution

This year's resolution
Is different from the rest
I'll mean what I say
And I'll do what I mean

No more wine
No more sweets
Cut out bread
Cut out meat

The gym will be my second home
I'm not going to gossip
I'm not going to shop
My credit card will be cut up

I'll be a better friend
A mother, a wife
Dedicate myself to others
For the rest of my life

This year's resolution
Is like none in the past
Because I'm going in wide eyed
With 20/20 vision

One of These Days

One of these days I'll…

Lose the weight

Call an old friend

Write the novel

Quit running so late

One of these days I'll…

Audition for a play

Cut my hair short

Try to like red wine

Mean what I say

One of these days I'll…

Be happy and content

Stop being afraid

Love who I am

Not cry over what I've spent

One of these days I'll…

March in a protest

Start my own business

Fight for a cause

Do what is best

One of these days I'll…

See my kids wed

Ride in a hot air balloon

Lie naked on a beach

Spend an entire day in bed

One of these days I'll…

Wash in the Dead Sea

Experience the Grand Canyon

Walk the Red Carpet

Visit the 50 states in an RV

One of these days I'll…

Stop blaming myself

Learn another language

Be a grandmother

Start taking care of my health

One of these days I'll…

Be a lot older

Wish I was younger

Not waited so long

Been a little bolder

One of these days…

The Beauty of a Fire

A radiant glow of a fire
Like a beautiful woman
Bewitches your mind
Pleasing to the eye
You can't look away
The warmth draws you in
Creating a desire
Taunting you to come closer
To feel its untamed power
Becoming part of the blaze
Swaying and moving with the flame
In a sensual dance
Higher and Higher
Faster and faster
Tantalizingly dangerous
Innately, we want to control it

When I Grow Up

When I grow up
I want to quit my job
Sleep in late
Drink coffee all morning and do my crosswords

When I grow up
I want play dates with my friends
Luncheons and spa days
Read good books and go on long walks

When I grow up
I want to travel
See the world
Take pictures of my journey

When I grow up
I won't fret about a thing
No schedule to follow
Nothing that I have to do

When I grow up
I 'll say what I want
Laugh until I cry
And act like a kid again

Life

Change

Change is all around us

Like a moving vehicle

Intertwining through the highways of life

Some embrace the steering wheel

With a grip of steel

White knuckled

Fearing which way to turn

While others speed along

Blowing through stop signs

Weaving in and out of cars

Missing where they need to go

The cruise controller sits back and relaxes

Taking in all the scenery

Not in a rush to get anywhere

Just enjoying the ride

Me, I'm a pump the brakes kind of driver

Always trying to control my speed

And afraid to change lanes

Default

Whose fault?

Your fault?

My fault?

Does anyone know?

Does anyone care?

Not me

Not you

Fresh start

Why not

So, restart

And default!

Life

Always changing
And never giving you a hint to why
People live it everyday
Sometimes wishing it away
Yet, we never want to lose it
For then, what would we have?
Life can take you up to the highest peak
Or down so far you don't know how to get up
But, it's always there
Waiting for you to capture its meaning
There are few to figure it out

Live

Live in the moment

Live in the second

Live in the hour

Live in the day

Live in the year

Live to laugh

Live to love

Live to help

Live to grow

Live for peace

Live for happiness

Live for wisdom

Live for others

Live for you

Live because you can

Live because you want

Live because you choose

Live because you dream

Live because

You do

People

Cheaters

You ever meet a cheater,

Who looked you in the eye?

Tried to be your friend

But you caught them in a lie?

They are smooth talking talkers

Swearing to the truth

Making you feel guilty

When you ask them for some proof

The crazy part is you believe them

You are caught in their story

Watching them gloat

In all their glory

My momma tried to tell me,

"Don't get caught up with a liar,

They'll use you and abuse you

Until you become the liar!"

Envy

What do they have

That you so desperately want?

House

Cars

Vacations

Power

Status

Could it be their happiness?

Contentment

Joy

Laughter

Confidence

Outwardly, no one could detect

Your discontentment from within

It is kept well hidden

At bay and tamed

Until good fortune befalls

On someone else

And not on you

Misery at its finest

It is alive

Like a rapid heart beat

The sting of heart burn

Is a reminder of this deadly sin

It is complex and complicated

Reasoning and rationalizing

Why this emotion consumes

Your mind, body, and soul

Would you sell your soul

For what your friend has acquired?

Or are they your foe?

Is it worth the price

To be the entitled one

That everyone is envious of?

You are not so unique

Another you comes along

Waiting to steal what is yours

Blinded by possessions

You didn't see it coming

Family

Did you ever wonder

How in the heck

You got the people in your family?

They don't look like you

They don't act like you

Did you ever wonder

If maybe, just maybe

You are in the wrong place

At the wrong time?

Meet Me in the Middle

Meet me in the middle
Let's resolve this constant dispute
Put aside the rising anger
Get into a good space

Meet me in the middle
Too much wasted time has gone by
I'm not asking for your approval
Or for you to switch sides

Meet me in the middle
Release that stubborn pride
My hand is extended
Grab ahold and I will pull you to the line

Meet me in the middle
It's ok, it's fine
I'm willing to compromise
And make adjustments where needed

At least meet me half-way

Religious

Angels

Never doubt the existence of Angels
They are never far away
 Watching over us
And shielding us from harm's way
With their silky white feathers
And musical voices
That we usually mistaken or brush away
It's the tightness in our chest
And a light touch against our face
Sending a signal, a warning, a push
Guiding us to safety
Never doubt the existence of Angels
They will always leave us a sign
Don't be surprised when a white feather
Appears in your path

God's Grace

Believe it

Receive it

Cherish it

Share it

Hang on to it

Expect it

Feel it

Love it

Know it

Be humbled by it

God's Grace

In the Middle of the Night

In the middle of the night
When no others are awake
I stare up at the ceiling
Waiting for day to break

In the middle of the night
Fears that loom inside me
Come to the surface of my mind
Fighting to be free

In the middle of the night
I seek rest for my soul
Petitioning forgiveness of sins
Yearning to feel whole

In the middle of the night
I hope, I dream, I pray
That the Good Lord above
Is listening to what I have to say

In the middle of the night
I hear that familiar voice
Telling me my prayers are answered
Relax, Receive and Rejoice!

My Saint

I was drawn to a place
So many years ago
My interest was sparked
By a black onyx ring
That I saw on the hand
Of a girl that I knew

She told me of this special locale
Hidden deep within the woods
That was created with a vision
To edify the young
And bring hope, wisdom and a new life
To those with none

A small humble woman
From a small village in France
Ventured far into the wilderness
To share the love of God
With everyone at hand

Some called her a visionary
Teacher, leader, mentor
An inspiration to others
Brave, fearless, courageous
Saint of Miracles
Servant of the Lord

Saint Mother Theodore Guerin

Servitude

To bow down to others
Doesn't make you weak
Or their slave
It heals your soul
And makes you the master
Of your own being

Speak Softly to Me

In the very far corner of my mind
When others are fast asleep
I lie in my bed awake
Thoughts in my head are racing

The stillness of the night
Covers me from the chill
My breathing starts to slow
Into a steady, rhythmic pattern

Gravity is pulling me down
I twist and turn, fighting myself
Reluctantly, my opponent bows out
Victory, I win

Today

Screw the Media

You are biased

You are fake

You can't be trusted

We want the facts

We want the truth

Where are your standards of journalism?

What happened to impartiality?

When did centrism become fair?

I'm not a fan

Play fair

Go left and right

Quit the downhill slide

Of promoting antagonistic tribes

Stop your tactics to influence the mass

And halt to create mayhem that sells

Do you really believe your audience is that absurd

To believe the lies you keep telling over and over again?

We don't need shaped

We don't need confusion

What we need is straight forward journalism

For the good and the whole of society

Street People

Do you ever think about the people living on the streets?

What are their names?

Who were they once before?

Wandering the streets

Nomads of the city

Invisible beings that are so visible

Others scurrying by them

Not giving them a thought

It's a strange dance

That most people don't take the extended hand

Or return the lonely smile

It is easier to ignore

And act like they don't exist

What are we afraid of?

Do we see something of ourselves

In the eyes of the homeless?

Are we afraid this too
Could become our fate?

They are bums

Lazy

Drug Addicts

Crazy

Criminals

Such easy words

That slide from our tongues

Cast upon others

Yet, their numbers alarmingly increase

Do you ever think about the people living on the streets?

Maybe you should

Too Much Technology Today

Not so long ago

There was a time

When people would actually talk to each other

Not through a text

Not through a tweet

Not by email

But they actually talked

With actual words

Face to face

Out loud

Not laugh out loud

LOL

How wonderful to hear the voice

Of your favorite person

See their facial expressions

A banter of words

A conversation

An argument

With a friend, a colleague, a lover

What fun having a gabfest

Of small talk, chit chat, gossip or just plain babble

No Snapchat

No Facebook

No Instagram

No TicToc

So, youth of today, listen up

Put down your iPhone

And let's talk for awhile

Under What Nation?

We live in a land

Where anything goes

You can do what you want

Say what you want

Believe what you want

Be what you want

And never really have to consider anyone else

We are a self-serving

Destructive machine

That keeps rolling and rolling

Rolling over others

That are in our way

United, you say?

The shooting

The lies

The greed

Stealing, cheating, killing

Judging someone for being themselves

We have 33 Constitutional Amendments

Ensuring us our freedoms

Giving us rights

But what's right anymore?

Burning our flag?

Kneeling during the Anthem?

Ridiculing our President?

Have we become so numb to moral consciousness

That we justify our heinous actions?

Mankind has not changed

Since the beginning of time

Same sins

Same wickedness

Different time

One nation

Under God

The home of the free

Land of the brave

I wonder what God thinks

When He looks down?

The "F" Word

F-Word, frankly, why do we use it?

Fricking, where did it come from?

F_ck, it's a four-letter word

F'ing, the same as love?

Frigging, where does it fit in our English language?

F-Bomb, noun, verb, adjective, interjection, adverb?

Eff, a time when it was the utmost obscene remark

F, yet it isn't so shocking to hear anymore

Freaking, freedom of speech

Flippin', Fourteenth Amendment protected

Fudge, take it at face value

WTF?

Women

Aging

Tuck it, suck it

Nip it, clip it

Who is that?

Looking back at me

There is something familiar

In the eyes

A sparkle, a light

Darting back and forth

Trapped in sunken hollows

Wondering where time went

Forget it, embrace it

Welcome it, screw it

It happens to the best of us

Each wrinkle with its own story

Sculpting our appearance

Chiseled face…

A mask of who we once were

Revealing the joys and the pains of our life

A photo of who we are

Maturing like a fine wine

Love it, take care of it

Cherish it, be proud of it

It's the only one we've got!

Dominique

What's behind those big dark eyes
And beautiful face
Iridescent and smooth
And your dazzling smile?
The tilt of your head
Placement of your arm
Color of your hair
Give no clue to who you are
Tall, lank, willowy
Cosmopolitan, bold
Queen of trends
The photo leaves you to ponder
Who is this mysterious being?
What road has she traveled?
What turns did she take?
Somewhere along the way
Traveling far and abroad
Did she find what she was searching for?
Did she find herself?
Aloof is a first impression
But it doesn't last long
As you push your way in
To her closed off walls
What do you see?
Free and alive

A playful heart

A creative soul

What's behind those big dark eyes?

Take a look and you will find

Wisdom, sensitivity, pain

A child-like twinkle

Dominique

Of the Lord

Belongs to God

The silver-moon enchantress

How to Love A Beautiful Woman

If you love a beautiful woman
And you treat her right
You will never have to worry
About an empty bed at night

If you love a beautiful woman
You must be creative in every way
To say the words she needs to hear
And say them every day

If you love a beautiful woman
You must be confident, sure and strong
Let her know you will be a man of your word
And admit when you are wrong

If you love a beautiful woman
Caress her body and kiss her skin
Alight a fire within her soul
And make her forget where she has been

If you love a beautiful woman
Make her laugh at every chance
Play her favorite love song
And slowly start to dance

If you love a beautiful woman
Express your sexual desire
Get wrapped up in her femininity
Set her body on fire

If you love a beautiful woman
Be her protector for life
She needs you to be her rock
And she will forever be your wife

Madness of a Menopausal Woman

I've been up all night
With not an hour of sleep
While my husband lay next to me
Making not a peep

I feel all sweaty
My nightgown is wet
Here come the cuss words
That I will later regret

My better half awakes
And scoots beside me
He tries to get fresh
But I work my way free

Now he's miffed
And I start to cry
"Why don't you want me?"
I really don't know why

Finally, I say
"I think I look fat"
He rolls his eyes
And asks, "What's the matter with that?"

I don't feel pretty
You don't find me sexy anymore
I'm bloated and puffy
Even getting out of bed is a chore

My hair is thinning
And I have dry skin
My breasts are saggy
I just want to be young again

Maybe I'm a little moody
And maybe my moods kind of swing
I am always tired
And I can't remember a thing!

"Now, now baby"
He says with a smile
"No need to get flustered,
Let's just sit for a while"

My first thought was to argue
My second thought was to flee
When suddenly my mind said
"Just let things be"

I love my husband dearly
And he may not be buff in a Speedo
But he still knows
How to fire up my libido!

So, women over fifty
You are hot, you are on fire
Reignite your "va va voom"
You are still much to desire!

Ode to a Gypsy Soul

Run wild, run free
My sweet gypsy girl
Never look back
Keep flowing through life
Seeking a place to stay for awhile
Until you're ill at ease

Dance wild, dance free
My sweet gypsy soul
Living on your wit
A drifter by nature
Deemed a modern-day nomad
With the wisdom of an old soul

Love wild, love free
My sweet gypsy soul
So much passion and so much lust
Simmering in your blood
Misunderstood and overtly complex
Not many afford a glimpse of your heart

Stay wild, stay free

My sweet gypsy soul

The universe is yours to seek

Never let your sparkle dim or your fire burn out

For this would be your curse

Remain an unpredictable disarray of beauty

Meet the Author

Kimberly McCaskey is a former elementary teacher from Indiana who lives in Annapolis, Maryland and is following her dream of writing poetry. Kim holds a Master's in Elementary Education, Administration and Supervision. She shared her love of poetry with her students throughout her 30-year career of teaching during National Poetry Month in April.

Kim and her husband own a home in Bluffton, South Carolina, but currently reside in Annapolis, Maryland with their Westie, Maggie. Kim's biggest accomplishment is her children, Kelsey and Tucker. When not working on her poetry, Kim loves cooking, yoga/working out, reading, history, crosswords and photography. Writing a children's poetry book is next on her bucket list!

www.ingramcontent.com/pod-product-compliance
Lightning Source LLC
Chambersburg PA
CBHW051838040426

42447CB00006B/597

9 781948 747622